Lincoln Land

W9-CAR-344

Chris, David, Grandma + Grand-
dad Rooks

Herman + Daphine Rooks

ABRAHAM LINCOLN

WISDOM & WIT

☞ *Edited by* LOUISE BACHELDER, *with*

Ilustrations by JEFF HILL

PETER PAUPER PRESS, INC.
WHITE PLAINS · NEW YORK

☞ Strange mingling of mirth and tears, of the tragic and grotesque, of cap and crown, of Socrates and Rabelais, of Aesop and Marcus Aurelius — Lincoln, the gentlest memory of the world.

ROBERT G. INGERSOLL

Lincoln, The Man

☞ Fellow citizens, I presume you all know who I am. I am humble Abraham Lincoln. I have been solicited by many friends to become a candidate for the Legislature. My politics are short and sweet, like the old woman's dance. I am in favor of the national bank; I am in favor of the internal improvement system and a high protective tariff. These are my sentiments and political principles. If elected, I shall be thankful; if not, it will be all the same. — [*First political speech given at Pappsville, Illinois, 1832, following a long dissertation by his opponent*]

☞ If any personal description of me is thought desirable, it may be said I am, in height, six feet four inches, nearly; lean in flesh, weighing, on an average, one hundred and eighty pounds; dark complexion, with coarse black hair, and grey eyes — no other marks or brands recollected.

☞ I don't know who my grandfather was; I am much more concerned to know what his grandson will be.

☞ My early life is characterized in a single line of Gray's *Elegy:* "The short and simple annals of the poor."

☞ All that I am, or hope to be, I owe to my angel mother. I remember her prayers, and they have always followed me. They have clung to me all my life.

☞ I never went to school more than six months in my life, but I remember how, when a mere child, I used to get irritated when anybody talked to me in a way I could not understand. . . . I can remember going to my little bedroom, after hearing the neighbors talk of an evening with my father, . . . trying to make out what was the exact meaning of some of their, to me, dark sayings.

I could not sleep, although I tried to, when I got on such a hunt for an idea until I had caught it; and when I thought I had got it, I was not satisfied until I had put it in language plain enough, as I thought, for any boy I knew to comprehend. This was a kind of passion with me, and it has stuck by me; for I am never easy now, when I am handling a thought, till I have bounded it north and bounded it south, and bounded it east and bounded it west.

☞ With educated people, I suppose, punctuation is a matter of rule; with me it is a matter of feeling. But I must say I have a great respect for the semicolon; it's a useful little chap.

☞ Upon the subject of education, not presuming to dictate any plan or system respecting it, I can only say that I view it as the most important subject which we as a people can be engaged in. That every man may receive at least a moderate education, and thereby be enabled to read the histories of his own and other countries, by which he may duly appreciate the value of our free institutions, appears to be an object of vital importance.

☞ I don't think much of a man who is not wiser today than he was yesterday.

☞ Others have been made fools of by the girls, but this can never with truth be said of me. I most emphatically, in this instance, made a fool of myself.

☞ I have now come to the conclusion never again to think of marrying, and for this reason — I can never be satisfied with anyone who would be blockhead enough to have me.

☞ Whatever woman may cast her lot with mine, should any ever do so, it is my intention to do all in my power to make her happy and contented; and there is nothing I can imagine that would make me more unhappy than to fail in the effort.

☞ I want in all cases to do right, and most particularly so in all cases with women.

☞ It is difficult to make a man miserable when he feels worthy of himself and claims kindred to the great God who made him.

☞ Every man is said to have his peculiar ambition. . . . I have no other so great as that of being truly esteemed of my fellow-men, by rendering myself worthy of this esteem. . . . I am young and unknown to many of you. I was born, and have ever remained, in the most humble walks of life. I have no wealthy or popular relations or friends to recommend me. My case is thrown exclusively upon the independent voters of the country; and, if elected, they will have conferred a favor upon me for which I shall be unremitting in my labors to compensate.

But if the good people, in their wisdom, shall see fit to keep me in the background, I have been too familiar with disappointments to be very much chagrined.

☞ I have endured a great deal of ridicule without much malice; and have received a great deal of kindness, not quite free from ridicule.

☞ I shall try to correct errors where shown to be errors, and I shall adopt new views as fast as they shall appear to be true views.

☞ The way for a young man to rise is to improve himself every way he can, never suspecting that anybody wishes to hinder him. Allow me to assure you that suspicion and jealousy never did help any man in any situation. There may sometimes be ungenerous attempts to keep a young man down; and they will succeed, too, if he allows his mind to be diverted from its true channel to brood over the attempted injury.

☞ I claim not to have controlled events, but confess plainly that events have controlled me.

☞ I have never had a policy. I have simply tried to do what seemed best each day, as each day came.

☞ In the earliest days of my being able to read, I got hold of a small book, Weems' *Life of Washington*. I remember all the accounts there given of the battlefields and struggles for the liberties of the country, . . . I recollect thinking then, boy even though I was, that there must have been something more than common that these men struggled for. I am exceedingly anxious that that thing — that something even more than national independence; that something that held out a great promise to all the people of the world to all time to come — I am exceedingly anxious that this Union, the Constitution, and the liberties of the people shall be perpetuated in accordance with the original idea for which that struggle was made. . . .

☞ I have never had a feeling, politically, that did not spring from the sentiments embodied in the Declaration of Independence.

☞ This habit of uselessly wasting time is the whole difficulty; it is vastly important to you, and still more so to your children, that you should break the habit. It is more important to them, because they have longer to live, and can keep out of an idle habit before they are in it, easier than they can get out after they are in. — [*Letter to John D. Johnston, stepbrother*]

☞ I think if I were you, in case my mind were not exactly right, I would avoid being *idle;* I would immediately engage in some business, or go to making preparations for it, which would be the same thing. [*Letter to Joshua Speed*]

☞ I never behold them [the heavens filled with stars] that I do not feel I am looking in the face of God. I can see how it might be possible for a man to look down upon the earth and be an atheist, but I cannot conceive how he could look up into the heavens and say there is no God.

☞ When any church will inscribe over its altar, as its sole qualification for membership, the Saviour's condensed statement of the substance of both law and Gospel, "Thou shalt love the Lord thy God with all thy heart, and with all thy soul and thy neighbor as thyself," that church will I join with all my heart and all my soul.

☞ In regard to this great book [*Bible*], I have but to say, it is the best gift God has given to men. All the good Saviour gave to the world was communicated through this book. But for it we could not know right from wrong. All things most desirable for man's welfare, here and hereafter, are to be found portrayed in it.

☞ I have never professed an indifference to the honors of official station; and were I to do so now, I should only make myself ridiculous. Yet I have never failed — do not now fail — to remember that in the republican cause there is a higher aim than mere office.

☞ If you are resolutely determined to make a lawyer of yourself, the thing is more than half done already. It is but a small matter whether you read *with* anybody or not. I did

not read with anyone. Get the books, and read and study them till you understand them in their principal features; and that is the main thing. It is of no consequence to be in a large town while you are reading. I read at New Salem, which never had three hundred people living in it. The *books*, and your *capacity* for understanding them, are just the same in all places.

☞ If I had to draw a pen across my record, and erase my whole life from sight, and I had one poor gift or choice left as to what I should save from the wreck, I should choose that speech [*The House Divided Against Itself*] and leave it to the world unerased.

☞ I say "try"; if we never try, we shall never succeed.

☞ If I were to try to read, much less answer, all the attacks made on me, this shop might as well be closed for any other business. I do the very best I know how — the very best I can; and I mean to keep doing so until the end. If the end brings me out all right, what is said against me won't amount to anything. If the end brings me out wrong, ten thousand angels swearing I was right would make no difference.

☞ I am not ashamed to confess that twenty-five years ago I was a hired laborer, hauling rails, at work on a flatboat — just what might happen to any poor man's son. I want every man to have a chance.

☞ I am always for the man who wishes to work.

☞ No, gentlemen; I have not asked the nomination, and I will not now buy it with pledges. If I am nominated and elected, I shall not go into the Presidency as the tool of this man or that man, or as the property of any factor or clique.

☞ I am very little inclined on any occasion to say anything unless I hope to produce some good by it.

☞ Nobody has ever expected me to be President. In my poor, lean lank face, nobody has ever seen that any cabbages were sprouting.

☞ I have been selected to fill an important office for a brief period, and am now, in your eyes, invested with an influence which will soon pass away; but should my Administration prove to be a very wicked one, or what is more probable, a very foolish one, if you, the people, are true to yourselves and the Constitution, there is but little harm I can do, thank God.

☞ I should be the most presumptuous blockhead upon this footstool if I for one day thought that I could discharge the duties which have come upon me, since I came to this place, without the aid and enlightenment of One who is stronger and wiser than all others.

☞ I am not at all concerned about that, that the Lord is on our side in this great struggle, for I know that the Lord is always on the side of the right; but it is my constant anxiety and prayer that I and this nation may be on the Lord's side.

☞ Some of our generals complain that I impair discipline and subordination in the army by my pardons and respites, but it makes me rested, after a hard day's work, if

I can find some good excuse for saving a man's life, and I go to bed happy as I think how joyous the signing of my name will make him [a deserter] and his family and his friends.

☞ I could not think of going into eternity with the blood of the poor young man [on sentry duty] on my skirts. It is not to be wondered at that a boy, raised on a farm, probably in the habit of going to bed at dark, should, when required to watch, fall asleep; and I cannot consent to shoot him for such an act.

☞ I have been shown in the files of the War Department a statement of the Adjutant-General of Massachusetts that you are the mother of five sons who have died gloriously on the field of battle. I feel how weak and fruitless must be any words of mine which should attempt to beguile you from the grief of a loss so overwhelming. But I cannot refrain from tendering to you the consolation that may be found in the thanks of the Republic they died to save. I pray that our heavenly Father may assuage the anguish of your bereavement, and leave you only the cherished memory of the loved and lost, and the solemn pride that must be yours to have laid so costly a sacrifice upon the altar of freedom. — [*Letter to Mrs. Bixby, November 21, 1864*]

☞ I am not accustomed to the use of the language of eulogy; I have never studied the art of paying compliments to women; but I must say, that if all that has been said by orators and poets since the creation of the world in praise of women were applied to the women of America, it would not do them justice for their conduct during this war. I will close by saying, God bless the women of America!

☞ In this sad world of ours, sorrow comes to all; and, to the young, it comes with bitterest agony, because it takes them unawares. The older have learned to ever expect it. . . .

☞ For one of my age, I have seen very little of the drama. . . . Some of Shakespeare's plays I have never read; while others I have gone over perhaps as frequently as any unprofessional reader. Among the latter are *Lear, Richard Third, Henry Eighth, Hamlet,* and especially *Macbeth.* I think nothing equals *Macbeth.* It is wonderful. Unlike you gentlemen of the profession [*letter to James H.*

Hackett, actor], I think the soliloquy in *Hamlet* commencing "O, my offence is rank" surpasses that commencing "To be, or not to be." But pardon this small attempt at criticism.

☞ I desire so to conduct the affairs of this administration that if at the end, when I come to lay down the reins of power, I have lost every other friend on earth, I shall at least have one friend left, and that friend shall be down inside of me.

☞ It is no pleasure to me to triumph over anyone.

☞ I am very sure that if I do not go away from here a wiser man, I shall go away a better man, from having learned here what a very poor sort of a man I am.

☞ I cannot understand why men should be so eager after money. Wealth is simply a superfluity of what we don't need.

☞ Many free countries have lost their liberty, and ours may lose hers; but if she shall, be it my proudest plume, not that I was the last to desert, but that I never deserted her.

☞ Die when I may, I want it said of me, by those who know me best, that I always plucked a thistle and planted a flower when I thought a flower would grow.

☞ I have said nothing but what I am willing to live by, and, if it be the pleasure of Almighty God, to die by.

Lincoln, The Philosopher

☞ Human nature will not change. In any future great national trial, compared with the men of this, we shall have as weak and as strong, as silly and as wise, as bad and as good.

☞ Important principles may and must be flexible.

☞ Truth is generally the best vindication against slander.

☞ If you once forfeit the confidence of your fellow citizens, you can never regain their respect and esteem. It is true that you may fool all the people some of the time; you can even fool some of the people all the time; but you can't fool all the people all the time.

☞ Among freemen there can be no successful appeal from the ballot to the bullet, and

. . . they who take such appeal are sure to lose their case and pay the cost.

☞ Labor is prior to, and independent of, capital. Capital is only the fruit of labor, and could never have existed if labor had not first existed.

☞ Stand with anybody that stands right. Stand with him while he is right, and part with him when he goes wrong.

☞ Gold is good in its place, but living, brave, patriotic men are better than gold.

☞ Let every man remember that to violate the law is to trample on the blood of his father, and to tear the charter of his own and his children's liberty.

☞ When one is embarrassed, usually the shortest way to get through with it is to quit talking or thinking about it, and go at something else.

☞ It is not the qualified voters, but the qualified voters who choose to vote, that constitute the political power of the State.

☞ All creation is a mine, and every man a miner. The whole earth, and all within it, upon it, and round about it, including himself, in his physical, moral and intellectual nature, and his susceptibilities, are the infinitely various "leads," from which man, from the first, was to dig out his destiny. In the beginning the mine was unopened, and the miner stood naked and knowledgeless upon it.

☞ Nothing should ever be implied as law which leads to unjust or absurd consequences.

☞ In this and like communities, public sentiment is everything. With public sentiment nothing can fail; without it, nothing can succeed. Consequently he who molds public sentiment goes deeper than he who enacts statutes or pronounces decisions. He makes statutes and decisions possible or impossible to be executed.

☞ Writing, the art of communicating thoughts to the mind through the eye, is the greatest invention of the world. Its utility may be conceived by the reflection that to it we owe everything which distinguishes us from savages. Take it from us, and the Bible, all history, all science, all government, all commerce, and nearly all social intercourse, go with it.

☞ When an end is lawful and obligatory, the indispensable means to it are also lawful and obligatory.

☞ What constitutes the bulwark of our own liberty and independence? It is not our frowning battlements, or bristling seacoasts, our army and navy. These are not our reliance against tyranny. All of those may be turned against us without making us weaker for the struggle. Our reliance is in the love of liberty which God has planted in us. Our defense is in the spirit which prized liberty as the heritage of all men, in all lands everywhere. Destroy this spirit and you have planted the seeds of despotism at your own doors.

☞ Let us at all times remember that all American citizens are brothers of a common country, and should dwell together in the bonds of fraternal feeling.

☞ Let reverence for the laws be breathed by every American mother to the lisping babe that prattles on her lap; let it be taught in schools, seminaries, and in colleges; let it be written in primers, spelling books and in almanacs; let it be preached from the pulpit, proclaimed in legislative halls, and enforced in courts of justice. And, in short, let it become the political religion of the nation.

☞ Universal idleness would speedily result in universal ruin.

☞ There are two ways of establishing a proposition. One is by trying to demonstrate it upon reason; and the other is, to show that great men in former times have thought so and so, and thus to pass it by the weight of pure authority.

☞ I believe each individual is naturally entitled to do as he pleases with himself and the fruits of his labor, so far as it in no wise interferes with any other men's rights.

☞ A tendency to melancholy . . . let it be observed, is a misfortune, not a fault.

☞ The people know their rights, and they are never slow to assert and maintain them, when they are invaded.

☞ Whenever this [slavery] question shall be settled, it must be settled on some philosophical basis. No policy that does not rest upon philosophical public opinion can be permanently maintained.

☞ I believe it is an established maxim in morals that he who makes an assertion without knowing whether it is true or false is guilty of falsehood, and the accidental truth of the assertion does not justify or excuse him.

☞ We know nothing of what will happen in future, but by the analogy of past experience.

☞ Wisdom and patriotism, in a public office, under institutions like ours, are wholly inefficient and worthless, unless they are sustained by the confidence and devotion of the people.

☞ It is as much the duty of government to render prompt justice against itself, in favor of citizens, as it is to administer the same between private individuals.

☞ If we have patience, if we restrain ourselves, if we allow ourselves not to run off in a passion, I still have confidence that the Almighty, the Maker of the Universe, will, through the instrumentality of this great and intelligent people, bring us through this as He has through all the other difficulties of our country.

☞ Let not him who is houseless pull down the house of another, but let him work diligently and build one for himself, thus by example assuring that his own shall be safe from violence when built.

☞ The better part of one's life consists of his friendships.

☞ The loss of enemies does not compensate for the loss of friends.

☞ How miserably things seem to be arranged in this world! If we have no friends, we have no pleasure; and if we have them, we are sure to lose them, and be doubly pained by the loss.

☞ Great distance in either time or space has wonderful power to lull and render quiescent the human mind.

☞ Surely God would not have created such a being as man, with an ability to grasp the infinite, to exist only for a day! No, no, man was made for immortality.

☞ How true it is that "God tempers the wind to the shorn lamb," or in other words, that he renders the worst of human conditions tolerable, while He permits the best to be nothing better than tolerable.

☞ A capacity and taste for reading gives access to whatever has been discovered by others. It is the key, or one of the keys, to the already solved problems. And not only so; it gives a relish and facility for successfully pursuing the unsolved ones.

☞ No men living are more worthy to be trusted than those who toil up from poverty — none less inclined to take or touch aught which they have not honestly earned.

☞ Extemporaneous speaking should be practiced and cultivated. It is the lawyer's avenue to the public.

☞ No man is good enough to govern another man without that other's consent.

☞ This is a world of compensations; and he who be no slave must consent to have no slave. Those who deny freedom to others deserve it not for themselves; and, under a just God, cannot long retain it.

☞ If a man is honest in his mind, you are pretty safe in trusting him.

☞ A universal feeling whether well or ill-founded, cannot be safely disregarded.

☞ The strongest bond of human sympathy, outside of the family relation, should be one uniting all working people, of all nations, and tongues, and kindreds.

☞ Always bear in mind that your own resolution to succeed is more important than any other one thing.

☞ The leading rule for the lawyer, as for the man of every other calling, is diligence. Leave nothing for tomorrow which can be done today.

☞ Character is like a tree and reputation like its shadow. The shadow is what we think of it; the tree is the real thing.

☞ The world has never had a good definition of the word liberty, and the American people, just now, are much in want of one. We all declare for liberty; but in using the same *word* we do not all mean the same *thing*. With some the word liberty may mean for each man to do as he pleases with himself, and the product of his labor; while with others the same word may mean for some men to do as they please with other men, and the product of other men's labor. Here are two, not only different, but incompatible things, called by the same name, liberty. And it follows that each of the things is, by the respective parties, called by two different and incompatible names — liberty and tyranny.

☞ The shepherd drives the wolf from the sheep's throat, for which the sheep thanks the shepherd as a *liberator*, while the wolf denounces him for the same act as the destroyer of liberty, especially as the sheep was a black one. Plainly the sheep and the wolf are not agreed upon a definition of the word liberty; and precisely the same difference prevails today among us human creatures. . . .

☞ This is the one hundred and tenth anniversary of the birthday of Washington.

We are met to celebrate this day. Washington is the mightiest name of earth — long since mightiest in the cause of civil liberty, still mightiest in moral reformation. On that name a eulogy is expected. It cannot be. To add brightness to the sun or glory to the name of Washington is alike impossible. Let none attempt it. In solemn awe pronounce the name, and in its naked, deathless splendor leave it shining on.

☞ At what point then is the approach of danger to be expected? I answer if it ever reach us it must spring up amongst us; it cannot come from abroad. If destruction be our lot, we must ourselves be its author and finisher. As a nation of free men, we must live through all time or die by suicide.

☞ Bless all the churches, and blessed be God who, in this our great trial, giveth us the churches.

☞ The man does not live who is more devoted to peace than I am, but it may be necessary to put the foot down firmly.

☞ In the right to eat the bread . . . which his own hand earns, he [the negro] *is my equal and the equal of Judge Douglas, and the equal of every living man.*

☞ My paramount object in this struggle is to save the Union, and is not either to save or destroy slavery. If I could save the Union without freeing any slave, I would do it; and if I could do it by freeing all the slaves, I would do it; and if I could save it by freeing some and leaving others alone, I would also do that.

☞ War, at the best, is terrible, and this war of ours, in its magnitude and in its duration, is one of the most terrible. It has deranged business, totally in many localities, and partially in all localities. It has destroyed property and ruined homes; it has produced a national debt and taxation unprecedented, at least in this country; it has carried mourning to almost every home, until it can almost be said that the "heavens are hung in black."

☞ The probability that we may fail in the struggle ought not to deter us from the support of a cause we believe to be just.

☞ Slavery is founded in the selfishness of man's nature — opposition to it in his love of justice.

☞ As I would not be a *slave*, so I would not be a *master*. This expresses my idea of democracy. Whatever differs from this, to the extent of the difference is no democracy.

☞ The dogmas of the quiet past are inadequate to the stormy present.

☞ It has been said of the world's history hitherto that might makes right. It is for us and for our time to reverse the maxim, and to say that right makes might.

☞ I hold that while man exists it is his duty to improve not only his own condition, but to assist in ameliorating mankind . . . I am for those means which will give the greatest good to the greatest number.

☞ The true rule, in determining to embrace or reject anything, is not whether it have any evil in it, but whether it have more of evil than of good. There are few things wholly evil or wholly good.

☞ The power of hope upon human exertion and happiness is wonderful.

Lincoln, The Wit

☞ I laugh because I must not cry.

☞ I have not permitted myself, gentlemen, to conclude that I am the best man in the country; but I am reminded in this connection of a story of an old Dutch farmer, who remarked to a companion once that it was not best to swap horses when crossing a stream.

☞ If you call a tail a leg, how many legs has a dog? Five? No; calling a tail a leg don't *make* it a leg.

☞ Men are not flattered by being shown that there has been a difference of purpose between the Almighty and them.

☞ I never encourage deceit; and falsehood, especially if you have got a bad memory, is the *worst* enemy a fellow can have. The fact is, truth is your truest friend, no matter what the circumstances are. Notwithstanding this copy-book preamble, my boy, I am inclined to suggest a *little prudence*.

☞ The lady bearer of this says she has two sons who want to work. Set them at it if possible. Wanting to work is so rare a want that it should be encouraged.

☞ I can make a brigadier-general in five minutes, but it is not easy to replace a hundred and ten horses.

☞ I think perhaps it might be wise to hand this letter from me, in to your good uncle through his room window *after* he has had a *comfortable dinner*, and watch its effect from the top of the pigeon-house.

☞ "A drop of honey catches more flies than a gallon of gall." So with men. If you would win a man to your cause, first convince him that you are his sincere friend. Therein is a drop of honey which catches his heart, which, say what he will, is the highroad to his reason. . . .

☞ If you make a bad bargain, hug it all the tighter.

☞ We better know there is fire whence we see much smoke rising than we could know it by one or two witnesses swearing to it. The witnesses may commit perjury, but the smoke cannot.

☞ War does not admit of holidays.

☞ By general law, life and limb must be protected, yet often a limb must be amputated to save a life; but a life is never wisely given to save a limb.

☞ His [man's] first discovery was the fact that he was naked; and his first invention was the fig-leaf apron. This simple article, the apron made of leaves, seems to have been the origin of clothing — the one thing for which nearly half of the toil and care of the human race has ever since been expanded.

☞ History is not history unless it is the truth.

☞ It is better only sometimes to be right, than at all times to be wrong.

☞ A jury too often has at least one member more ready to hang the panel than to hang the traitor.

☞ The Presidency, even to the most experienced politicians, is no bed of roses.

☞ God selects his own instruments, and sometimes they are queer ones; for instance, He chose me to steer the ship through a great crisis.

☞ In law it is good policy to never *plead* what you *need not*, lest you oblige yourself to *prove* what you *cannot*.

☞ Reports are often false, and always false when made by a knave to cloak his knavery.

☞ Bad promises are better broken than kept.

☞ Military glory — that attractive rainbow that rises in showers of blood, that serpent's eye that charms to destroy.

☞ A nation may be said to consist of its territory, its people and its laws. The territory is the only part which is of certain durability.

☞ Your note, requesting my "signature with a sentiment," was received, and should have been answered long since, but that it was mislaid. I am not a very sentimental man; and

40

the best sentiment I can think of is, that if you collect the signatures of all persons who are no less distinguished than I, you will have a very undistinguishing mass of names.— [*Congressman Lincoln's reply to a man who asked for his autograph — 1849*]

☞ Human action can be modified to some extent, but human nature cannot be changed.

☞ The plainest print cannot be read through a gold eagle.

☞ It is said an Eastern monarch once charged his wise men to invent an aphorism to be ever in view, and which should be true and appropriate in all times and situations. They presented him the words, "And this, too, shall pass away."

☞ Few can be induced to labor exclusively for posterity; and none will do it enthusiastically. Posterity has done nothing for us.

☞ Ready are we all to cry out and ascribe motives when our own toes are pinched.

☞ As for being President, I feel like the man who was tarred and feathered and ridden out of town on a rail. To the man who asked him how he liked it, he said, "If it wasn't for the honor of the thing, I'd rather walk."

☞ Towering genius disdains a beaten path.

☞ I could as easily bail out the Potomac River with a teaspoon as attend to all the details of the army.

☞ I don't want to quarrel with him, — to call him a liar, — but when I come square up to him, I don't know what else to call him, if I must tell the truth out.

☞ I was not very much accustomed to flattery, and it came the sweeter to me. I was rather like the Hoosier with the gingerbread, when he said he reckoned he loved it better than any other man, and got less of it.

☞ An honest laborer digs coal at about seventy cents a day, while the President digs abstractions at about seventy dollars a day. The coal is clearly worth more than the abstractions, and yet what a monstrous inequality in the prices.

43

☞ There is something so ludicrous in promises of good or threats of evil a great way off as to render the whole subject with which they are connected easily turned into ridicule:

"Better lay down that spade you are stealing, Paddy; if you don't you'll pay for it at the day of judgment."

"Be the powers, if ye'll credit me so long, I'll take another jist."

☞ If the Lord gives a man a pair of cowardly legs, how can he help their running away with him?

☞ When I am getting ready for an argument, I spend one third of my time thinking about what I am going to say, and two thirds about what my opponent will say.

☞ When a man hears himself somewhat misrepresented, it provokes him — at least, I find it so with myself; but when misrepresentation becomes very gross and palpable, it is more apt to amuse him.

☞ I leave it to my audience, — if I had another face to wear, do you think I would wear this one? — [*Lincoln had been called a "two-faced man" by Douglas*]

☞ Young lawyer, don't shoot too high — aim lower, and the common people will understand you. They are the ones you want to reach — at least, they are the ones you ought to reach. The educated and refined people will understand you, anyway. If you aim too high, your idea will go over the heads of the masses, and only hit those who need no hitting.

☞ When we were the political slaves of King George, and wanted to be free, we called the maxim that "all men are created equal" a self-evident truth, but now, when we have grown fat, and have lost all dread of being slaves ourselves, we have become so greedy to be *masters* that we call the same maxim a "self-evident lie."

☞ Every man has his own peculiar and particular way of getting at and doing things, and he is often criticized because that way is not the one adopted by others. The great idea is to accomplish what you set out to do.

☞ By the way, do you know I am a military hero? Yes, sir, in the days of the Black Hawk

War, I fought, bled, and came away. Speaking of General Cass's career reminds me of my own. I was not at Stillman's defeat, but I was about as near it as Cass to Hull's surrender; and like him I saw the place very soon afterwards. It is quite certain I did not break my sword, for I had none to break, but I bent my musket pretty badly on one occasion. . . . If General Cass went in advance of me picking whortleberries, I guess I surpassed him in charging upon the wild onion. If he saw any live, fighting Indians, it was more than I did, but I had a good many bloody struggles with the mosquitoes, and although I never fainted from loss of blood, I can truly say that I was often very hungry.

☞ Quarrel not at all. No man resolved to make the most of himself can spare time for personal contention. Still less can he afford to take all the consequences, including the vitiating of his temper and the loss of self-control. Yield larger things to which you can show no more than equal right; and yield lesser ones, though clearly your own.

Better give your path to a dog than be bitten by him in contesting for the right. Even killing the dog would not cure the bite.

☞ True patriotism is better than the wrong kind of piety.

☞ Long experience has shown that nothing short of an actual demand of the money will expose an adroit peculator. Ask him for reports, and he will give them to your heart's content; send agents to examine and count the money in his hands, and he will borrow of a friend, merely to be counted and then returned, a sufficient sum to make the sum square. Try what you will, it will all wait till you demand the money; then, and not till then, the truth will come.

☞ I indicated no wish or purpose of my own; I simply expressed my *expectation.* Cannot the Judge perceive the distinction between a *purpose* and an *expectation?* I have often expressed an expectation to die, but I have never expressed a *wish* to die.

☞ Books serve to show a man that those original thoughts of his aren't very new, after all.

☞ My father taught me to work, but not to love it. I never did like to work, and I don't deny it. I'd rather read, tell stories, crack jokes, talk, laugh — anything but work.

☞ There is a vague popular belief that lawyers are necessarily dishonest. I say vague, because when we consider to what extent confidence and honors are reposed in and conferred upon lawyers by the people, it appears improbable that their impression of dishonesty is very distinct and vivid. Yet the impression is common, almost universal. Let no young man choosing the law for a calling for a moment yield to the popular belief — resolve to be honest at all events; and if in your own judgment you cannot be an honest lawyer, resolve to be honest without being a lawyer. Choose some other occupation rather than one in the choosing of which you do, in advance, consent to be a knave.

☞ He who does something at the head of one regiment will eclipse him who does nothing at the head of a hundred.

☞ Equality in society beats inequality, whether the latter be of the British-aristocratic sort or of the domestic-slavery sort.

☞ Consciences differ in different individuals.

☞ I believe I shall never be old enough to speak without embarrassment when I have nothing to talk about.

☞ He reminds me of the man who murdered both his parents, and then when sentence was about to be pronounced, pleaded for mercy on the grounds that he was an orphan.

☞ I hold that if the Almighty had ever made a set of men that should do all the eating and none of the work, He would have made them with mouths only and no hands; and if He had ever made another class that He intended should do all the work and no eating, He would have made them with hands only and no mouths.

☞ I happen, temporarily, to occupy the White House. I am a living witness that any one of your children may look to come here as my father's child has.

☞ Why, if any one else had been President and had gone to Richmond, I would have been alarmed; but I was not scared about myself a bit.

☞ If the head of Lee's army is at Martinsburg, and the tail of it on the Plank road between Fredericksburg and Chancellorsville, the animal must be very slim somewhere. Could you [General Hooker] not break him?

☞ The Lord prefers common-looking people. That is the reason He makes so many of them.

☞ He can compress the most words into the smallest ideas of any man I ever met.

☞ Broken eggs cannot be mended.

☞ Better to remain silent and be thought a fool than to speak out and remove all doubt.

☞ Happy day when — all appetites controlled, all poisons subdued, all matter subjected — mind, all conquering mind, shall live and move, the monarch of the world. Glorious consummation! Hail, fall of fury! Reign of reason, all hail!

Excerpts from His Speeches

A House Divided

☞ "A house divided against itself cannot stand." I believe this government cannot endure permanently half slave and half free. I do not expect the Union to be dissolved. I do not expect the house to fall — but I do expect it will cease to be divided. It will become all one thing or all the other. Either the opponents of slavery will arrest the further spread of it, and place it where the public mind shall rest in the belief that it is in the course of ultimate extinction; or its advocates will push it forward, till it shall become alike lawful in all the states, old as well as new — North as well as South — [*From speech accepting nomination to oppose Senator Stephen A. Douglas who won re-election, June 16, 1858*]

☞ Now, and here, let me guard a little against being misunderstood. I do not mean to say we are bound to follow implicitly in whatever our fathers did. To do so would be to discard all the lights of current experience — to reject all progress — all improvement. What I do say is, that if we would supplant the opinions and policy of our fathers in any case, we should do so upon evidence so conclusive, and argument so clear, that even their great authority, fairly considered and weighed, cannot stand; and most surely not in a case whereof we ourselves declare they understood the question better than we. . . .

. . . . .

Wrong as we think slavery is, we can afford to let it alone where it is, because that much is due to the necessity arising from its actual presence in the nation; but can we, while our votes will prevent it, allow it to spread into the National Territories and to overrun us here in these Free States? If our sense of duty forbids this, then let us stand by our duty, fearlessly and effectively. Let us be diverted by none of those sophistical contrivances wherewith we were so industriously plied and be-labored — contrivances such as groping for some middle ground between the right and the wrong, vain as the search for a man who should be neither a living man nor a dead man — such as a policy of "don't care" on a question about which all true men do care.

.   .   .   .   .

Neither let us be slandered from our duty by false accusations against us, nor frightened from it by menaces of destruction to the Government nor of dungeons to ourselves. *Let us have faith that Right makes Might, and in that faith, let us, to the end dare to do our duty as we understand it.* — [*From address at Cooper Institute, New York, February 27, 1860*]

FAREWELL ADDRESS

☞ My Friends: No one, not in my situation, can appreciate my feeling of sadness at this parting. To this place, and the kindness of these people, I owe everything. Here I have lived a quarter of a century, and have passed from a young to an old man. Here my children have been born, and one is buried. I now leave, not knowing when or whether ever I may return, with a task before me greater than that which rested upon Washington. Without the assistance of that Divine Being who ever attended him, I cannot succeed. With that assistance, I cannot fail. Trusting in Him who can go with me, and remain with you, and be everywhere for good, let us confidently hope that all will yet be well. To His care commending you, as I hope in your prayers you will commend me, I bid you an affectionate farewell.—[*Complete speech, Springfield, Illinois, February 11, 1861*]

ULTIMATE JUSTICE OF THE PEOPLE

☞ I hold, that in contemplation of universal law, and of the Constitution, the Union of these States is perpetual. . . . It is safe to assert that no government proper, ever had a provision in its organic law for its own termination. . . .

One party to a contract may violate it — break it, so to speak; but does it not require all to lawfully rescind it? . . .

Physically speaking, we cannot separate. We cannot remove our respective sections from each other, nor build an impassable wall between them. . . .

This country, with its institutions, belongs to the people who inhabit it. . . .

Why should there not be a patient confidence in the ultimate justice of the people? Is there any better or equal hope in the world? . . .

While the people retain their virtue and vigilance, no administration, by any extreme of wickedness or folly, can very seriously injure the government in the short space of four years. . . .

In *your* hands, my dissatisfied fellow countrymen, and not in *mine*, is the momentous issue of civil war. The government will not assail *you*. You can have no conflict, without being yourselves the aggressors. *You* have no oath registered in Heaven to destroy the government, while *I* shall have the most solemn one to "preserve, protect and defend" it.

I am loathe to close. We are not enemies but friends. We must not be enemies. Though passion may have strained, it must not break our bonds of affection. The mystic chords of memory, stretching from every battle-field, and patriot grave, to every living heart and hearth stone, all over this broad land, will yet swell the chorus of the Union, when again touched, as surely they will be, by the better angels of our nature. — [*From First Inaugural Address, Washington, March 4, 1861*]

We Cannot Escape History

☞ Fellow citizens, we cannot escape history. We and this administration will be remembered in spite of ourselves. No personal significance can spare one or another of us. The fiery trial through which we pass will light us down, in honor or dishonor, to the latest generation. . . . We — even we here — hold the power and bear the responsibility. In giving freedom to the slave, we assure *freedom to the free* — honorable alike in what we give and what we preserve. We shall nobly save or meanly lose the last, best hope of earth. — [*From Annual Message to Congress, December 1, 1862*]

Slaves . . . Shall Be Free

☞ . . . And, by virtue of the power and for the purpose aforesaid, I do order and declare that all persons held as slaves within said designated States and parts of States, are, and henceforward shall be, free; and that the Executive Government of the United States, including the military and naval authorities thereof, will recognize and maintain the freedom of said persons.

And I hereby enjoin upon the people so declared to be free, to abstain from all violence, unless in necessary self-defense; and I recommend to them, that in all cases, when allowed, they labor faithfully for reasonable wages.

And I further declare and make known that such persons of suitable condition will be received into the armed service of the United States. . . .

And upon this act, sincerely believed to be an act of justice, warranted by the Constitution, upon military necessity, I invoke the considerate favor of the Almighty God.— [*From Emancipation Proclamation, Washington, January 1, 1863*]

GETTYSBURG ADDRESS

☞ Fourscore and seven years ago our fathers brought forth upon this continent a new nation, conceived in liberty, and dedicated to the proposition that all men are created equal. Now we are engaged in a great civil war, testing whether that nation, or any nation so conceived and so dedicated, can long endure. We are met on a great battlefield of that war. We have come to dedicate a portion of that field as a final resting-place for those who here gave their lives that that nation might live. It is altogether fitting and proper that we should do this. But in a larger

sense we cannot dedicate, we cannot conse-
crate, we cannot hallow this ground. The
brave men, living and dead, who struggled
here, have consecrated it far above our poor
power to add or detract. The world will little
note, nor long remember, what we say here;
but it can never forget what they did here. It
is for us, the living, rather to be dedicated
here to the unfinished work which they who
fought here have thus far so nobly advanced.
It is rather for us to be here dedicated to the
great task remaining before us, that from
these honored dead we take increased devotion to that cause for which they gave the last
full measure of devotion; that we here highly
resolve that these dead shall not have died in
vain; that this nation, under God, shall have a
new birth of freedom, and that government
of the people, by the people, and for the people, shall not perish from the earth. — [*Complete speech, Dedication of the National
Cemetery at Gettysburg, November 19,
1863*]

WITH MALICE TOWARD NONE

☞ The Almighty has his own purposes. . . .
Fondly do we hope — fervently do we pray —
that this mighty scourge of war may speedily

pass away. Yet, if God wills that it continue, until all the wealth piled by the bond-man's two hundred and fifty years of unrequited toil shall be sunk, and until every drop of blood drawn with the lash, shall be paid by another drawn with the sword, as was said three thousand years ago, so still it must be said; "the judgments of the Lord, are true and righteous altogether."

With malice toward none; with charity for all; with firmness in the right, as God gives us to see the right, let us strive on to finish the work we are in; to bind up the nation's wounds; to care for him who shall have borne the battle, and for his widow, and his orphan — to do all which may achieve and cherish a just and lasting peace, among ourselves, and with all nations. — [*From Second Inaugural Address, Washington, March 4, 1865*]

NOW HE BELONGS TO THE AGES
Edwin M. Stanton